A Basic Guide To
BADMINTON

An Official U.S. Olympic Committee Sports Series

The U.S. Olympic Committee

Griffin Publishing

Editorial Statement

In the interest of brevity, the Editors have chosen to use the standard English form of address. Please be advised that this usage is not meant to suggest a restriction to, nor an endorsement of, any individual or group of individuals, either by age, gender, or athletic ability. The Editors certainly acknowledge that boys and girls and men and women of every age and physical condition are actively involved in sports and we encourage everyone to enjoy the sports of his or her choice.

10 9 8 7 6 5 4 3 2 1

ISBN 1-882180-76-3

Griffin Publishing

544 W. Colorado Street
Glendale, California 91204
Telephone: 1-818-244-1470

U.S. Olympic Committee

One Olympic Plaza
Colorado Springs, Colorado 80909
Telephone: 1-719-632-5551

Manufactured in the United States of America

Acknowledgments

PUBLISHER	**Griffin Publishing Group**
PRESIDENT	**Robert M. Howland**
DIR. / OPERATIONS	**Robin L. Howland**
MANAGING EDITOR	**Marjorie L. Marks**
WRITER	**Jeff Klemzak**
BOOK DESIGN	**Mark M. Dodge**
COORDINATOR	**Bryan K. Howland**
CONSULTING EDITORS	**Richard D. Burns, Ph.D.**
	Don Chew
USOC	**United States Olympic Committee**
PRESIDENT	**William J. Hybl**
EXEC. DIRECTOR	**Richard D. Shultz**
DEP. SEC'Y. GENERAL	**John Krimsky, Jr.**
USA BADMINTON	**Terry Madden**
	Marc Whitney
	Michael Rodriguez
PHOTOS	**USA Badminton**
	Dave Black
	Thanarat Hongcharoen
	Wade Nash
	Warren Emerson
	Stabler Photography
	Dick McCoy/Thumbs Up
COVER PHOTO	**USA Badminton**
ATHLETE ON COVER	**Kevin Han, a member of the 1996 U.S. Olympic Badminton Team and to whom the publisher extends special appreciation.**

Special thanks for the suggestions of badminton official Paisan Rangsikitpho, coaches Vicki Toutz and Pat McCarrick, to Eric McMullin, Holly Peters, Danny King, Jr., Mike Colias of USA Badminton, and especially to Paul Pawlaczyk.

The United States Olympic Committee

The U.S. Olympic Committee (USOC) is the custodian of the U.S. Olympic Movement and is dedicated to providing opportunities for American athletes of all ages.

The USOC, a streamlined organization of member organizations, is the moving force for support of sports in the United States that are on the program of the Olympic and/or Pan American Games, or those wishing to be included.

The USOC has been recognized by the International Olympic Committee since 1894 as the sole agency in the United States whose mission involves training, entering and underwriting the full expenses for the United States teams in the Olympic and Pan American Games. The USOC also supports the bid of U.S. cities to host the winter and summer Olympic Games or the winter and summer Pan American Games and, after reviewing all the candidates, votes on and may endorse one city per event as the U.S. bid city. The USOC also approves the U.S. trial sites for the Olympic and Pan American games team selections.

On behalf of the United States Olympic Committee,

Welcome to the
Olympic Sports Series

We are extremely pleased to inaugurate the Olympic Sports Series. I feel this unique series will encourage parents, athletes of all ages and novices who are thinking about a sport for the first time, to get involved with the challenging and rewarding world of Olympic sports.

This series of paperback books covers both summer and winter sports, features Olympic history and basic sports fundamentals, and encourages family involvement. Each book includes information on how to get started in a particular sport, including equipment and clothing; rules of the game; health and fitness; basic first aid; and guidelines for spectators. Of special interest is the information on opportunities for senior citizens, volunteers and physically challenged athletes. In addition, each book is enhanced by photographs and illustrations and a complete, easy-to-understand glossary.

Because this family-oriented series neither assumes nor requires prior knowledge of a particular sport, it can be enjoyed by all age groups. Regardless of an individual's level of sports knowledge, playing experience or athletic ability, this official U.S. Olympic Committee Sports Series will encourage understanding and participation in sports and fitness.

The purchase of these books will assist the U.S. Olympic Team. This series supports the Olympic mission and serves importantly to enhance participation in the Olympic and Pan American games.

John Krimsky, Jr.
Secretary General

Contents

An Athlete's Creed

The most important thing in the Olympic Games is not to win but to take part, just as the most important thing in life is not the triumph but the struggle. The essential thing is not to have conquered but to have fought well.

These famous words, commonly referred to as the Olympic Creed, were once spoken by Baron Pierre de Coubertin, founder of the modern Olympic Games. Whatever their origin, they aptly describe the theme behind each and every Olympic competition.

1

A Brief History of a New Olympic Sport

Many Americans only know badminton as a picnic sport, a leisurely game played on warm summer afternoons cooled by pitchers of iced tea. To those who play it competitively, however, badminton is far from leisurely. Badminton is a sport that requires a quick hand, keen eye, and clever footwork.

Badminton, like baseball, has been described as a game of inches. The court is relatively small and a skilled player must use the narrow confines to his or her advantage. An Olympic champion can swat the shuttle (sometimes referred to as a shuttlecock or birdie) over the net at a frantic 200 miles per hour. The opponent, by the flick of a wrist, can return the shuttle at a deceptively slower speed and, relying on the element of surprise, score a point in the process.

History

The history of badminton, although incompletely documented, is known to have been played in

India under the name of Poona. It was brought to England, probably by returning army officers, around 1870, and was first played at the estate of the Duke of Beaufort in his hometown of Badminton. The Duke entertained a great deal, thereby fostering the popularity of badminton among the British upper classes. The early playing courts were designed in the shape of an hourglass.

Photo by Jeff Klemzak
Badminton is a high-energy sport

The hourglass shape was used because the Duke's badminton room had doors that opened inward from the walls at the net area. It was decided to narrow the court at the net so that guests could come and go without disturbing play. It wasn't until 1901, after the death of the Duke, that the present rectangular court dimensions were adopted.

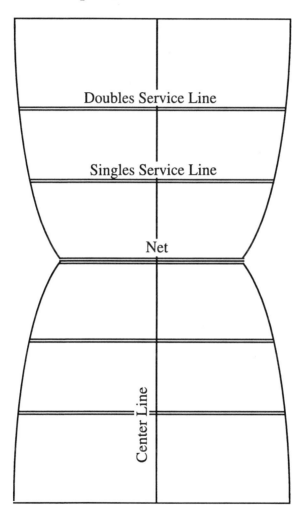

The Duke's hourglass-shaped court

The first badminton club in the United States was formed in New York in 1878 and soon became a popular weekend getaway for society's elite. The roster of member names included Vanderbilts, Roosevelts and Rockefellers. Badminton matches were held on several courts, most of which were decorated with brightly colored banners and pennants.

Men wore tuxedos, cumbersome Prince Albert coats and patent leather dancing shoes, while women appeared with elaborately arranged hair and attired in the long, bulky dresses that were the style of that era.

Shuttlecocks were made of chicken feathers and varied greatly in size. Early badminton racquets, made of wood, were heavy and unwieldy. The clothing and the equipment combined to limit the style of play, making overhand smashes and subtle drop shots all but impossible.

Badminton became the rage in the United States during the Depression years of the thirties, owing its popularity—at least in part—to the antics of one Hugh Forgie. Forgie came to New York from Canada in 1934 as a member of a touring amateur hockey team. He soon found that he could do better as a badminton instructor. He teamed up with British trick shot artist Ken Davidson a few years later and the two barnstormed around the country giving electrifying exhibitions of badminton skill.

During the 1950s, Forgie combined his hockey and badminton skills to tour the country with the Ice Capades. He was to badminton what the Harlem Globe Trotters were to basketball. In one of his routines, Forgie cleverly speed-skated around the net returning his own shots, mixing athletic grace with burlesque humor, to the great delight of crowds wherever he appeared.

The popularity of badminton did not escape the attention of Hollywood. Many movie stars, including James Cagney, Pat O'Brien, Bette Davis, Boris Karloff and Ginger Rogers were players, as well as the former Olympic swimming champion, Johnny Weismuller, who became the movies' "Tarzan."

Every other year, in even numbered years, badminton players throughout the world meet on a national basis to compete in the world championships held by the International Badminton Federation (IBF). Male players compete for the Thomas Cup, while women vie for the Uber Cup. Both prizes are named for famous badminton competitors of the past, Sir George Thomas and the fine mixed doubles player, Mrs. H.S. Uber.

Badminton has recently begun to make a comeback in the United States, recapturing its former popularity. The USA Badminton (USAB), in a study released in 1993, states that more than 1.2 million Americans play badminton regularly and that more than 750,000 Americans regard badminton as their favorite sport.

Photo by Wade Nash
Indonesia's Hermawan Susanto hits a hot smash over the net

While badminton is regaining ground in the United States, including the development of its own top athletes, the best players in the world currently come from both Southeast and East Asia—where badminton has been immensely popular for some time.

Championship players, such as Alan Budi Kusuma and Susi Susanti, Olympians from Indonesia, are held in the same high esteem by the public in their homeland as are baseball star Ken Griffey Jr. and figure skating sensation Kristi Yamaguchi in the United States. Susi Susanti, the Indonesian singles player, became badminton's first Olympic champion when she defeated South Korea's Bang Soo Hyun in the 1992 Olympic games in Barcelona. Susanti also became the first Olympic gold medal winner from Indonesia and is revered there as a national heroine.

The popularity that badminton champions enjoy in Far East nations has never translated into the financial rewards that many western athletes enjoy. The top badminton stars met in Bangkok in December 1994 in the Grand-Prix final, competing for a fraction of the purse offered to tennis players who appeared at Wimbeldon during the same year. Ardy Wiranata, for example, the men's champion badminton singles player, won less than $20,000, while Pete Sampras, who won the men's tennis final, received more than $500,000.

Photo by Jeff Klemzak

Jumping for a power play

To remedy this disparity, the IBF recently signed
a contract with the Star Television Group, which

broadcasts exclusively to Asian countries. An affiliation with a western satellite group also is expected.

Badminton in the Olympics

Badminton arrived as an Olympic sport at the Barcelona games in 1992. It is estimated that the matches were viewed on television by more than 1.1 billion people worldwide. More than 170 million viewers tuned into one series of matches alone.

In two previous Olympiads, the 1972 games in Munich and the 1988 games in Seoul, badminton was played as a demonstration sport. It is interesting to note that although no gold or silver medals were to be awarded in Seoul, the seats for the badminton matches were among the first to be sold out.

Badminton athletes who qualified for the 1996 Olympic Games were chosen through an international selection process. No United States trials or playoffs were held during the one-year qualifying period from April 1, 1995 to March 31, 1996. During that time, athletes competed in at least eight international tournaments and earned world player rankings. At the end of the qualifying period, the Olympians were chosen from an official International Badminton Federation (IBF) computer ranking list of world players.

Medals Summary
1995 Pan American Games
Buenos Aires, Argentina, March 12-16, 1995

Men's Singles
Gold—Jamie Dawson (CAN)
Silver—Iain Sydie (CAN)
Bronze—Kevin Han (USA)
Bronze—Mario Carulla (PER)

Women's Singles
Gold—Denyse Julien (CAN)
Silver—Iian Deng (CAN)
Bronze—Beverly Tang Choon (TRI)
Bronze—Kathy Zimmerman (USA)

Men's Doubles
Gold—Iain Sydie/Anil Kaul (CAN)
Silver—Kevin Han/Thomas Reidy (USA)
Bronze—Paul Leyow/Roy Paul (JAM)
Bronze—Jaimie Dawson/Darryll Yung (CAN)

Women's Doubles
Gold—Sian Deng/Denyse Julien (CAN)
Silver—Milaine Cloutier/Robbyn Hermitage (CAN)
Bronze—Linda French/Erika Von Heiland (USA)
Bronze—Ann French/Kathy Zimmerman (USA)

Mixed Doubles
Gold—Darryll Yung/Denyse Julien (CAN)
Silver—Anil Kaul/Sian Deng (CAN)
Bronze—Mike Edstrom/Linda French 22(USA)
Bronze—Paul Leyow/Terry Leyow (JAM)

The IBF was then responsibile for selecting the world's top 176 players and, adding a few more from the reserve list, plus some wild card entries, reached a total of 192 athletes to compete in Atlanta. From the 192 candidates, thirty-six players were chosen for the men's singles event, thirty-six more for women's singles, and forty each for men's doubles, women's doubles, and mixed doubles.

Photo courtesy of USOC

The 1996 U.S. Olympic Badminton Team:
Top—USA National Team Coach Goran Sterner, Kevin Han
Bottom—Erika Von Heiland, Athletes Advisory Council
Representative Ann French, Linda French

Within the selection process the IBF set forth a few conditions: Each of the five IBF continental bodies (Asia, Africa, Europe, Oceana and Latin

America) must be represented. No more than three athletes per event from any one country are permitted and the United States, as the host country, was guaranteed two spots in the badminton events.

In January 1995 the USAB, in anticipation of the 1996 Atlanta Games, established a full-time resident athlete training program at the Olympic Training Center in Colorado Springs, Colorado. America's finest badminton athletes now would have access to a state-of-the-art facility providing strength and speed programs within a consistent training schedule.

Also, as a prelude to the 1996 Olympics, badminton debuted at the March 1995 Pan American Games in Buenos Aires, Argentina. The athletes from the United States did very well, winning medals in several events. The U.S. team proved to be talented and resourceful, showing strength in every division

The 1995 Olympic Festival, held in Boulder, Colorado, featured many of the American Olympic hopefuls, among them Kevin Han, Tom Reidy, and Kathy Zimmerman.

The 1996 Olympic badminton competition held at Georgia State University immediately captured the imagination of the fans and kept the crowd highly entertained for the entire week of action. Badminton events were consistently sold out long before the matches began. This reflected the keen revival of interest in top grade badminton competition among American fans. Even though no United States player advanced beyond the first round, fan support was high. As the American players appeared on the court the chanting of "U-S-A, U-S-A" resounded loudly from the stands.

U.S. Olympic Badminton Team warming up in Atlanta

The gold medal in the men's singles competition was taken by Denmark's Poul-Erik Hoyer-Larsen, who blitzed all opponents, never failing to win a game in every match. Hoyer-Larsen, who had won the Thomas Cup competition at Hong Kong earlier in the year, defeated the 1992 Olympic gold medalist, Indonesia's Allan Budi Kusuma and the 1995 World Champion, Heryanto Arbi along the way. Facing the Chinese champion and

No. 1 world-ranked Dong Jiong in the finals, Hoyer-Larsen went to work with relentless accuracy as he outmaneuvered his opponent to win the final two games and the gold.

1996 Olympic Medalists

Men's Singles
Gold—Poul-Erik Hoyer-Larsen (DEN)
Silver—Dong Jiong (CHN)
Bronze—Rashid Sidek (MAS)

Women's Singles
Gold— Bang Soo Hyun (KOR)
Silver—Mia Audina (INA)
Bronze—Susi Susanti (INA)

Men's Doubles
Gold—Ricky Subagja and Rexy Mainaky (INA)
Silver—Cheah Soon Kit Yap Kim Hock (MAS)
Bronze—Antonius/Denny Kantono (INA)

Women's Doubles
Gold—Ge Fei/Gu Jun (CHN)
Silver—Gil Young Ah/Jang Hye Ock (KOR)
Bronze—Qin Yiyuan/Tang Yongshu (CHN)

Mixed Doubles
Gold—Kim Dong Moon Gil Young Ah (KOR)
Silver—Park Joo Bong/Ra Kyung Min (KOR)
Bronze—Liu Jianjun/Sun Man (CHN)

The women's singles competition was won by Korea's Bang Soo Hyun who capitalized on the mysterious underachievement of top-seeded Ye Zhaoying, the Chinese champion who dropped out in the quarterfinals.

Photo by Jim Stabler

**Korea's Bang Soo Hyun lofts a
drop shot over the net**

Bang Soo Hyun, who won the 1992 silver medal at Barcelona, turned the tables on her old rival in the semifinals, 1992 gold medalist Susi Susanti, before easily defeating 16-year-old phenomenon in the finals, Indonesia's Mia Audina, 11-6 and 11-7 to win the gold. Easily the most talked about match was the men's doubles final that featured top-seeded Indonesians Ricky Subagja and Rexy Mainaky, who faced the second-seeded Malaysian team of Cheah Soon Kit and Yap Kim Hock. Spectators who were in Atlanta that day remember an extremely high-spirited contest that became more intense with each point.

The Malaysian team appeared to be on their way to an upset and a gold medal as they dominated the first game with a series of kill shots, 15-5. The Indonesians came right back in the second to take a long lead, then almost lose it before coming back again to squeak by 15-13. In the third and final contest, the gold medal was decided by the Indonesian team, which competed vigorously to achieve a 15-12 triumph, leaving in their wake a throng of limp and exhausted fans.

During the final game of the hard-fought match, *Washington Post* columnist, David Broder, who was present as a spectator, wrote of one particularly intense 90-second rally that it was "one of the supreme sports spectacles of my entire life."

International Competition

With the growing popularity of badminton worldwide, especially since the end of World War

Photo by Jim Stabler
**Poul-Erik Hoyer-Larsen on the victory stand
in Atlanta**

II, several international tournaments appear on the calendar each year. In 1996 alone, the International Badminton Federation (IBF) listed more than fifty badminton events that were to be held in various parts of the world. This number did not include the Olympic Games at Atlanta.

Championship badminton competition, as we recognize it today, began in Great Britain in 1899 when the All-England Championships were first played. These games crowned the unofficial world badminton champions in the five major categories of play (men's singles and doubles, women's singles and doubles, and mixed doubles). Since 1977, however, the All-England Championships have been replaced by the official World Badminton Championships. This championship series is rich with badminton history, having showcased such stars as the perennial American women's singles champion of the 1950s and 1960s, Judy Devlin (who later became known as Mrs. Judy Hashman) and the Indonesian men's singles champion, the beloved Rudy Hartono. These games are played every odd year and are held in conjunction with the Sudirman Cup.

Dick Sudirman, for whom the Sudirman Cup is named, was known as the father of Indonesian badminton. Sudirman, who was a championship player for many years, served the IBF in several capacities, most notably as vice president. The Sudirman Cup is awarded to the winners of the world mixed team badminton championship. The teams from participating countries play five matches (men's singles and doubles, women's singles and doubles, and mixed doubles) against each other. The winners of the last four Sudirman Cups have been China, Korea (twice), and Indonesia, while the United States has finished no closer than twenty-first, which it achieved in 1989.

Photo by Jim Stabler

The men's doubles match between Malaysia and Indonesia (Atlanta, 1996) was one of the most rousing in recent memory

In 1993, the IBF, after some years of lobbying, finally convinced the Pan American Sports Organization (PASO) to include badminton in the 1995 Pan American Games. The United States Olympic Committee formulated a list of rules for players who wished to appear in the Pan American Games, among which is the requirement that the players be United States citizens, be competitors in the U.S. Open and in *at least* four other qualifying tournaments.

The Pan American Games are multi-sport events held every four years since 1951. As many as forty-one countries from North, South, and Central America participate. The 1995 games, held in Buenos Aires, Argentina, offered medals in thirty-seven sports. The United States badminton team was very successful, earning six medals (one silver and five bronze) among all five events. The 1999 Pan American Games will be played in the Canadian prairie city of Winnepeg, Manitoba.

American badminton players who wish to compete in events held in the United States have a very busy tournament schedule from which to choose. Competitive badminton has come a long way from the first USA Badminton Championship, which was played at the Naval Armory Pier in Chicago in 1937. From coast-to-coast, an abundance of championship badminton events are held every year. Among the leading U.S. tournaments are the Mid-Atlantic Classic and the Connecticut Open on the eastern seaboard, the Mile-High Challenge in Colorado, the St. Louis Classic, the California State Championships, and the Yonex U.S. Open, held in a different American city every year.

1995 Pan American Games
USA Badminton Team

Women:

Ann French, La Jolla, CA
Linda French, San Diego, CA
Joy Kitzmiller,* Manhattan Beach, CA
Erika Von Heiland, San Diego, CA
Alternate: Kathy Zimmerman,* Denver, CO

Men:

Mike Edstrom, Tempe, AZ
Kevin Han, Colorado Springs, CO
Ben Lee,* Daly City, CA
Tom Reidy, Colorado Springs, CO
Alternate: Christopher Hales,* Wooster, OH

*Alternates Zimmerman and Hales replaced Kitzmiller and Lee, who were unable to participate.

The athletes who qualify for these tournaments have dedicated themselves to practice, spending years honing their skills and making the sacrifices necessary to become top badminton players. Does hard work pay off? Just ask any one of the young men or women from any of the Olympic teams and you will hear an emphatic,"Yes"!

Erika Von Heiland

A one-time tennis star in her native Philippines, Erika turned to badminton and became an even bigger sensation. She represented the Philippines in international competition until her migration to the United States in 1985, where she now is one of the top-ranked female badminton players. Erika was added to the U.S. National Team in 1989 and by 1992 she was on her way to Barcelona where she represented the United States as a singles player and, with Linda French, participated on the women's doubles team.

Erika spent most of 1995 trying to qualify for the 1996 U.S. Olympic team and after compiling the necessary points in international competition, became a surprise entrant as part of the women's doubles team. Although the American team was eliminated in the first round, Erika's attitude was positive.

"Our triumph has truly been in our struggle to get here," she said of her Olympic experience.

Photo by Warren Emerson

Erika reaches for a drop shot

2

THE PROPER GEAR

During the early days of badminton, when society matrons and gentlemen moved stiffly about the court in heavy, restrictive clothing, the racquets were thickly framed, wooden objects. They were strung haphazardly and were far too cumbersome for clever, deceptive net play. By contrast, the equipment and clothing available today is strong and light, facilitating a game of speed and power.

Modern badminton players can sustain rallies that exhibit amazing agility and stamina. For example, in the 1992 U.S. Open finals, one men's doubles rally endured for eighty-seven shots, but took only sixty-three seconds to complete! Of course, modern athletes benefit from advances in coaching and nutrition that have improved the quality of the game. Also, one cannot underestimate the importance of advancements in design and manufacturing technology that have advanced all aspects of court equipment available to today's badminton players.

Choosing a Racquet

A contemporary badminton racquet is light and maneuverable, weighing a mere three-and- one-half ounces, and is constructed of aluminum, steel, ceramic and graphite elements. Modern racquets, despite their lightweight design, are very strong and resistant to warping.

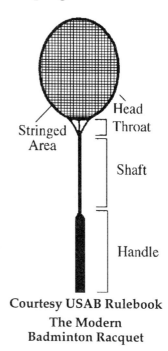

Courtesy USAB Rulebook
The Modern
Badminton Racquet

Regulations limit racuets to twenty-seven inches in length and nine inches in width.

Also, the head length is restricted to nine inches. A player testing a new racquet should take notice of the grip, the way the racquet feels as the arm is extended, as well as its balance. The flex (or stiffness) of a racquet is an important factor for players who wish to improve their skills.

Also, equal consideration must be given to the strings and their thickness, construction, proper installation and tension.

Strings

Racquet strings are available in two categories: natural gut and synthetic. Gut strings, although more expensive than those made from synthetic fibers, are generally preferred by experienced players. Natural gut string is made from bovine intestines and is more resilient than is synthetic, offering the player better shot control. Racquet strings are also available in various thicknesses, with the thinner-gauged filaments suggested for more advanced players.

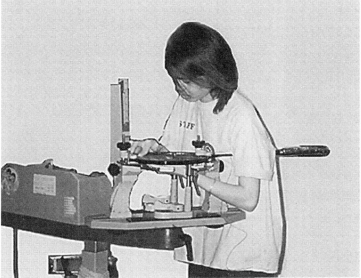

Photo by Jeff Klemzak

Restringing a racquet in a pro shop

Usually, thicker strings are more durable than the finer variety, but the thinner strings carry more energy to a shot and provide more playability. A knowledgeable badminton player will select the type of string that best suits his or her game and rely on the experience of a professional racquet stringer to fine-tune the racquet to the proper tension.

Among players of intermediate ability, finesse players keep their racquets strung looser (eighteen to nineteen pounds) than power players who usually prefer more tension on the strings. A more loosely strung racquet offers better control to the delicate shots that net players need. The top players, however, who use both finesse and power in their game, generally prefer more string tension (twenty-four to twenty-five pounds). Most badminton coaches suggest that a player restring a badminton racquet as often in one year as he or she plays in one week. If you play three times a week, replace the strings three times a year.

Badminton racquets should be stored in their covers when not in use and kept in a normal room-temperature environment. Avoid storing racquets in places where temperature fluctuations are extreme. It is never wise to store a badminton racquet in the trunk of a car.

A comfortable grip is essential for maintaining the integrity of a badminton racquet. Racquet grips often become worn from use and perspiration and, in such deteriorated condition, may slide from a player's grasp. Some players prefer to use temporary "over-grips" made from terry cloth or nonskid synthetic material, while others may wish to invest in a new professionally installed grip.

The Shuttlecock

One of the things that distinguishes badminton from tennis and other racquet sports is the use of the shuttlecock. Also known as the shuttle or bird, the shuttlecock must conform to certain standards. For a shuttle to be used in competition, it must be made of sixteen feathers attached to a cork base that is covered with leather. Shuttles are also available in nylon or plastic, but their use is generally restricted to practice sessions and backyard games.

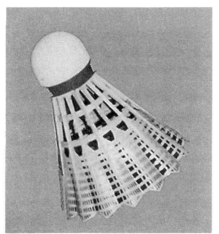

Photo by Jeff Klemzak
A synthetic shuttle for outdoor, amateur play

For centuries in Asian countries, white geese and ducks have been bred and raised for food. After these birds have been harvested, the feathers are saved and then sorted as to species—ducks in one pile, geese in another. They are further sorted into left wing and right wing feathers because an individual shuttle is made with feathers that must be faced in the same direction. Because only six or seven feathers from each wing are used in the manufacture of shuttlecocks, it takes six wings from three geese to produce two shuttles.

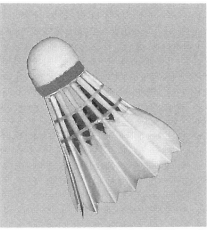

Photo by Jeff Klemzak
A feathered shuttle

It is recommended that the feathered shuttles be stored in tubes when not in use. Shuttles can be lightly steamed to keep them supple. Brittle feathers don't last very long in tournament play when struck repeatedly by aggressive badminton players. One suggestion is to quickly dip the shuttles in hot water while exposing the empty tube to the steam. Replace the shuttles in their tubes capping them immediately. This will keep the shuttles soft and pliable until put in use.

Because shuttle manufacturers are free to set their own standards as to "tournament quality," the USAB submits shuttles made by various manufacturers to rigorous testing before they can be approved for tournament play. The USAB tests the shuttles according to several criteria, including weight, number of feathers, and performance. According to the official USAB rules of play, Law 4.4 states that for the purpose of testing, the shuttle be struck with a "full underhand stroke," from the back boundary line. "The shuttle shall be hit at an upward angle" and travel over the net. A shuttle of "correct pace" will land no less than 530mm (1-1/2 feet) nor more than 990mm (3 feet) "short of the other back boundary line."

Clothing

According to *Badminton USA*, the official publication of the USAB, badminton tournament players in 1995 began to experiment with multicolored clothing. Displacing the traditional whites that had been standard badminton attire for many decades, players in the World Cup in Jakarta, Indonesia, and the World Grand Prix in Singapore wore brightly colored apparel with player's names on the backs.

The athletes were allowed to wear any color they chose, providing the clothing was "neither offensive nor distracting to the opposition," according to IBF Executive Director David Shaw. "We are looking at ways of improving our presentation and enlivening the game," he said.

Photo by Thumbs/Up
**Multicolored outfits are replacing the traditional whites—now
seldom-used in tournament play**

White tennis shoes or sturdily constructed court shoes are the footwear of choice for most tournament players. Gone are the days when ladies and gentlemen slid around the court in clumsy leather shoes. Many athletes use specially constructed orthotics (plastic inserts placed in shoes) for better arch support. With the heavy pounding that tournament players' feet must endure, quality, supportive footwear is a must.

RULES &
FUNDAMENTALS

Badminton is a game that can be played indoors or outdoors. However, at the competitive level, and certainly in the Olympics, the matches are held in an indoor arena. The court measures forty-four feet by twenty feet for doubles matches and forty-four feet by seventeen feet for singles. Courts include three feet of clearance space at the sides and six feet at the ends. The net measures two and one-half feet in width and is five-feet high at midcourt (five feet, one inch at the posts).

Scoring

A match is decided by the best two of three games. A game of badminton is won when one side scores fifteen points, except for women's singles, in which a game is defined by one side reaching eleven points. As in tennis and handball, only the side serving is entitled to score points. If the winner of a rally is the side out, that is, the side not serving, they score no points but win the right to serve.

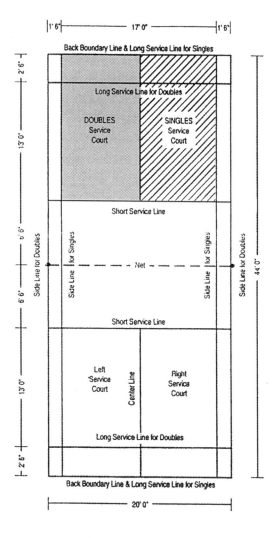

The Badminton Court

Scoring in badminton is similar to that of handball. Only one point is awarded to the server when a fault is committed by the side out.

Unlike tennis, however, the server is allowed only one opportunity to put the shuttle in play. In doubles competition *both* players have a chance at a serve before defaulting to the other side. Serving is diagonal and originates in the right-hand court. If a serve strikes the top of the net before going over, it is deemed legal and "in play" provided the shuttle arrives in the proper service court.

Photo by Thumbs/Up

Her racquet held ready for a comeback as her partner serves

The player serving the shuttle as well as the player receiving the service must keep both feet in bounds and stationary on the court. The server is not permitted any preliminary motions designed to throw his opponent off balance, such as feints or false starts. The shuttle must be below the server's waist as it is struck and it must be struck with an underhand motion. The racquet head must be below the server's hand. A fault is called if the receiver's partner returns a serve meant for the receiver.

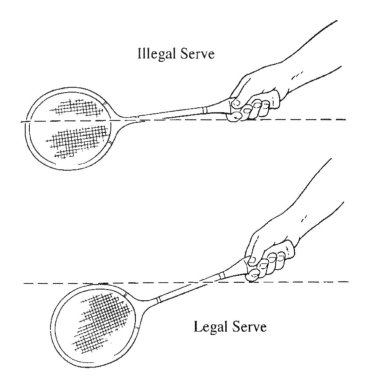

Illegal Serve

Legal Serve

For a serve to be legal, the racquet head must be below the hand

During play a fault is called if the shuttle falls outside the boundaries of the court, although if the shuttle strikes the boundary line it is determined to be "in." The shuttle is not permitted to go into, under, or through the net.

A player may not strike the shuttle more than once before returning it to the opponent. A fault is called if a player invades the opponent's court under the net with racquet or person and causes an obstruction. Players are not permitted to touch the net during play with racquet, body, or clothing.

As mentioned earlier, badminton uses a shuttle-cock rather than a ball, like other racquet sports, so it is important to note that the shuttle must not strike the court surface during the course of a rally.

Other Rules

Before play can commence, the winner of a coin toss chooses one of two available options. The winner may elect to either serve or receive, or may choose the end of the court from which play begins. The loser of the toss receives the remaining option.

Much as in a football game, where teams change the direction of play from one end of the field to another, badminton rules call for the players, during the course of the match, to change ends of the court. In a three-game match, the players move at the finish of the first game and prior to the start of the third game (if needed). In the third game—or if it is a one-game match—the players change ends when the leading score reaches six points in a game of eleven or eight points in a game of fifteen.

Photo by Thanarat Hongcharoen

Badminton officials in their chairs above the action

A "let" may be called by an umpire to halt play because of a number of occurrences. It is badminton's version of a "time-out" although the purpose of a "let" is not to give the players a breather, but to correct something that has gone wrong during the contest. When a "let" is called, the play since the last serve does not count and the serve is repeated. If the shuttle snags on the net during a rally and remains on top or gets caught in the net after passing over, a "let" is called. During a serve, a similar infraction would be deemed a "fault."

If during a service, the server and receiver are *both* called for a fault, the umpire will call a "let." A "let" will also be called if the server serves the shuttle before the receiver is deemed ready. Occasionally, a shuttle may disintegrate during a rally. If this happens, a "let" will be called. If a line judge is "unsighted," that is, blocked or otherwise prevented from viewing a play, and the umpire is unable to make a decision, a "let" is announced and the rally is replayed.

The rules of badminton require that play be continuous from the first serve of the contest until the match has been concluded. There are very few exceptions. In most tournament play a break of five minutes is allowed between the second and third game of a match, but under no circumstances is play suspended so that a player can regain his/her strength or to receive instructions from a coach or manager. Players may be disciplined for causing play to be suspended by interfering with the shuttle in play or behaving boorishly during the course of the contest.

Photo by Paul Pawlaczyk

World-renowned umpire Paisan Rangsikitpho at work in Atlanta at the 1996 Olympics

In response to these offenses, the umpire will issue a warning to the offender and fault the offender if a previous warning already has been issued. In cases of "flagrant and/or persistent offenses," the referee has the power to disqualify. If no referee is present, a "responsible official" is empowered to disqualify the offending party.

As mentioned earlier, badminton, unlike other racquet sports, uses a shuttlecock rather than a ball. It is important that the shuttle not strike the court surface during the course of a rally.

Badminton for the Disabled

Under the rules of badminton, provisions have been made for disabled players. The changes in the rules have been made to accommodate semi-ambulant people, those with crutches, prostheses, braces and other supports as well as changes for players who are confined to wheelchairs.

Disabled players are given a smaller court on which to compete, and the rule that requires a diagonal serve, from the left service court to the opponent's right, for example, has been waived. Also, the additional line that bisects the court between the short service line and the long service line also becomes the rear boundary line (see the figures below).

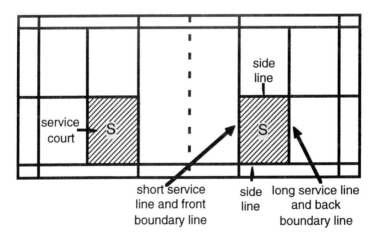

Court layout for disabled players (singles)

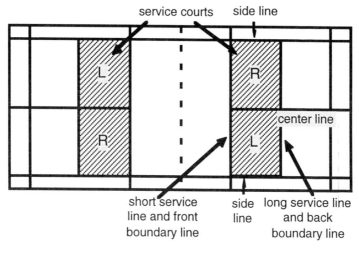

Court layout for disabled players (doubles).
Players must serve and receive from the same service court
throughout the game. The rule requiring diagonal
service is waived

Some years ago, in Los Angeles, several ambulatory badminton players attempted to play a game of badminton while confined to wheelchairs. It was through their efforts that the above rules changes were adopted for disabled players. Sources queried for information about disabled badminton players, however, can recall no tournaments that have been specifically held for disabled players.

Setting

If the score is tied late in the game at "thirteen-all," the player who was the first to arrive at thirteen has the option of extending the game by "setting" to five. This player can choose to set in order to stall the momentum of the opponent who has just tied the score. This means that the game would be decided at eighteen instead of fifteen points.

Points in Game	Score Tied at	Game May Be Set to
11	9-all	3 points, making a 12-point game
11	10-all	2 points, making a 12-point game
15	13-all	5 points, making a 18-point game
15	14-all	3 points, making a 17-point game

Courtesy *USBA 60th Jubilee Fact Book*, 1996

Also, in a game at "fourteen-all," the player first to arrive at fourteen may set the game at three, extending it to seventeen points. In women's singles competition, a game may total twelve points by setting at "nine-all" for a three-point extension or at "ten-all" for two. Setting, however, is not permitted in handicap competition.

Officials

Four types of officials are used to define and enforce the rules in a badminton match, although all four need not be present at any given contest. The referee is the official in charge of the tournament or event. If an umpire is used, he/she is in charge of the match, the court, and the immediate surroundings. The umpire reports to the referee. A service judge determines any service faults, and a line judge indicates whether the shuttle is "in" or "out" of bounds. A good line judge seldom misses a line call and will make his decision, "in" or "out," firmly and with authority.

The umpire is expected to enforce the rules of badminton and to call a "fault" or "let" if necessary. He does not permit any appeal by the players. The umpire not only makes decisions about bounced shuttles, net infractions and unsportsmanlike conduct, but keeps the audience and players informed of the score. An umpire will announce at the beginning of a game, for example, "Love-all, play" (with love meaning zero), or during the course of the match, "Game point, fourteen" or "Game point, ten."

Shuttle landed in.   Shuttle landed out.   Judge was
                                                    unsighted.

Courtesy *USBA 60th Jubilee Fact Book*, 1996
Line Judge Signals

Beginning a game, the umpire will inquire of the players, "Are you ready?" and communicate with them further from his chair during the play that follows. The umpire may command, "Play a let," or "You must not interfere with the speed of the shuttle." A careless player may be reminded by the umpire that, "You are standing in the wrong court," or to a player who seems to be holding up play before a serve that, "Play must be continuous." At the end of play the umpire will announce the name of the winning player or team, and in an international event the name of the country also is announced.

In the past, the International Badminton Federation (IBF), working with the International Olympic Committee, has assembled the most highly regarded officials in the world to judge the Olympic Games. Olympic play is closely scrutinized, showing respect for the athletes who have sacrificed and worked so hard to be there.

4

A Spectator's View

The level of competition that one finds in tournament play is vastly different from that found in the friendly, backyard version of badminton familiar to most people. As in any sport that has evolved from recreational beginnings, competitive badminton involves strategies and techniques that have grown up with the game, eventually becoming essential to the success of the top-notch players.

Singles

In singles play, the object is to make the opponent move back and forth on the court by mixing one's shots and forcing the opponent to commit an error. A singles rally opens with an underhand serve. The players may volley across the net with sidearm drives, moving each other around, looking for openings and weaknesses. At this point, a player may attempt to win a point by "setting up" the opponent, driving him to the rear of the court with a powerful overhead smash, then coming back with a drop shot, badminton's version of the change-up pitch, which drops over the net, just out of reach of the charging opponent.

Photo by Wade Nash
The singles player covers the whole court

Another popular singles strategy is the "waiting game."A player may choose to keep the rally alive with long, overhead "clear" shots confining his opponent to midcourt, patiently waiting for the opponent to become frustrated and commit an error. A frustrated player, even if he possesses superior skills, may take his best shot in the wrong part of the court, hitting the shuttle into the net or out of bounds, thus giving up a point to a less-skilled opponent.

One of the delightful aspects of badminton is the variety of different shots one can make from a given position. For example, from midcourt a player can choose a hard smash, an underhand drop shot, or even an overhead clear shot that drives the opponent to the back of the court.

Photo by Jeff Klemzak

Fielding a backcourt clear shot

A good badminton player can administer these shots with a supple wrist, flicking a shot away from an opponent who may be moving in the wrong direction.

A shot often seen in tournament play is the "overhead clear," a defensive shot that is also deceptive. At first, it appears to be a smash, but instead sends the shuttle to the rear of the opponent's court, setting him up for a drop shot.

The backhand shots can be particularly difficult for newer players to master, yet, with practice they become important strokes to add to one's repertoire.

A backhand shot is essential

For most younger players the difficulty in executing the backhand lies in taking the shot with the back toward the net. The backhand clear is often a "set up" shot that eventually results in a deceptive drop shot. The backhand smash is considered by many to be the most difficult shot to complete, especially in tournament badminton where the stakes are often high and room for error is slim.

Another shot worth mentioning is the round-the-head shot. Unique to badminton, this shot is completed in a manner inferred from its name. The player swats the shuttle from the backhand side, using a forehand grip, facing the net or the opponent as he swings. It can be a very effective, deceptive maneuver.

Doubles

In doubles play, the strategy of the team is to strike the shuttle *down* to their opponents, forcing them to return the shuttle in an *upward* motion as it crosses the net. The teams are aligned offensively with one player at the net and the other delivering drives and smashes from the backcourt. On defense, both players stay to the back, covering both sides of the court, ready to shift positions as the game accelerates.

Doubles play relies less on shot selection strategy than it does on player position and overall team strategy. The action in a doubles match generally centers around the net, featuring drives, smashes and drop shots, as opposed to a singles match, which offers more in the way of long, clear shots. Doubles teammates who have a well-coordinated position strategy, rotating up and back as the situations dictate, can often defeat a team that possesses better racquet skills but more plodding footwork.

Mixed Doubles

The 1996 Olympics featured a new badminton event, mixed doubles, which joined the existing events of men's singles and doubles and women's singles and doubles. The mixed doubles event is the only Olympic contest, apart from the equestrian events, that offers direct competition between men and women.

Photo courtesy of Wade Nash
A Swedish mixed doubles team recovers to make a point

The key to winning mixed doubles matches, most experts agree, is the strategy employed by the teams to neutralize the usual disparity in strength between the competing men and women. The woman generally plays up, near the short service line (see court diagram, Chapter 3), covering the near sidelines and the net. She is responsible for returning the half-court shots and drives. Her male partner roams the backcourt starting fifteen feet or so behind the net and is responsible for the power shots; i.e., the hard drives and smashes.

Most mixed doubles matches showcase a lot of cross-court driving and maneuvering, with players scoring points with deceptive half-court and net shots. The long "clear" shots that one sees in singles matches, shots that force a player away from the net, are generally avoided in mixed doubles because the front-back player positioning defeats their purpose.

Audiences can look for some teams to attempt to disrupt the woman-up/man-back defense positioning by hitting higher, deeper serves to the female, pushing her away from the net, bringing the male partner forward. A deep smash return shot with the male defenseman drawn in too close can result in confusion for the defense and a quick score for the cagier team.

Linda French

Linda has competed to date in two Olympic games, at Barcelona in 1992 and at Atlanta in 1996. Since badminton's medal status was only attained in those two competitions, Linda is recognized as a USA Badminton pioneer. A long-time championship player, Linda has been the U.S. women's doubles champion five times (with several partners including her eventual Olympic partner, Joy Kitzmiller) and has been part of the U.S. mixed doubles championships seven times.

On the international circuit, Linda was the 1995 bronze medalist at the Pan American Games, has appeared on five World Championship teams, six U.S. Uber Cup teams and was the 1995 Puerto Rican Open women's singles and doubles champion.

Prior to her appearance at the summer games in Barcelona, Spain, Linda was required to play in a minimum of eight international tournaments (with partner Kitzmiller).

"We probably played in 15 or 20 (tournaments)", said French of her appearances in such places as London, Paris, Copenhagen and Jamaica. "I probably would have felt the travel was worthwhile even if I hadn't made the team, but it was definitely worthwhile now."

Photo by Dave Black

Linda drives one over the net

Photo by Wade Nash

Staying fit on the badminton court

5

BADMINTON AS A FITNESS PROGRAM

One way badminton players attain and retain fitness is simply by playing badminton. It is estimated that in a typical two-game singles match, players run an average of one mile, covering practically every square inch of the court. Badminton is not just good exercise—it's an aerobic sport, and much more. By lunging, running, and jumping, players develop strong muscles and quick reflexes as they race around the court.

Badminton is probably the least understood sport in the United States in terms of the physical demands required of its participants. As an example, let's compare the performance of Boris Becker, the German tennis champion in the 1985 Wimbeldon finals, with those of Han Jian of China and Denmark's Morten Frost in the 1985 World Badminton Championships held in

Calgary, Canada. The Becker-Curren match, which was eventually won by Becker, consumed three hours and eighteen minutes with the ball actually in play for eighteen minutes. The tennis match was comprised of 299 rallies and 1,004 individual strokes with an average of 3.4 shots per rally. Jian and Frost, on the badminton court, played fewer rallies but took an incredible 1,972 shots, almost twice the number of the match at Wimbledon! The tennis players took only 5.1 shots per minute, while in Calgary Jian and Frost, competing in Calgary, took an astounding 25.9 shots per minute. Quite a workout!

The physical demands made of badminton players was further demonstrated when it was revealed that Jian and Frost ran four miles during their match, while the Wimbledon finalists covered only two miles. The point is not to diminish the sport of tennis but, rather, to indicate the intensity inherent in high-level badminton competitions. A badminton player not only must practice in order to achieve an enormous number of shots during a rally, but he or she must train so that the body is in shape for such strenuous activity. A good player needs a quick racquet, quick footwork, and the stamina necessary to keep going, shot after shot.

Tennis vs. Badminton: Statistics Don't Lie

The speed and stamina required for badminton competition are far greater than for any other racquet sport. At the 1985 All-England (Tennis) Championships, Boris Becker defeated Kevin Curren 6-3, 6-7, 7-6, 6-4. At the 1985 World Badminton Championships in Calgary, Canada, Han Jian of China defeated Morten Prost of Denmark 14-18, 15-10, 15-8. The following is a statistical comparison of those matches.

	Tennis	Badminton
Time	3 hrs. 18 min.	1 hr. 16 min.
Ball/Shuttle in Play	18 min.	37 min.
Match Intensity*	9%	3%
Rallies	299	146
Shots	1,004	1,972
Shots Per Rally	3.4	3.5
Distance Covered	2 miles	4 miles

Note that the badminton players competed for half the time, yet ran twice as far and hit nearly twice as many shots.

*The actual time the ball/shuttle was in flight, divided by the length of the match

Training

Apart from actually playing badminton to get in shape, some training exercises are suggested as well. Running or jogging before a badminton match is a good way to warm up. Running increases blood flow to the entire body, including the arms, thus reducing the risk of unnecessary muscle pulls. Also, a jogging or running program is a great way to build the stamina an athlete needs for a competitive badminton match.

Photo by Jeff Klemzak

Strength training is important to many badminton players

Some badminton players have enjoyed the benefits of a weight training program, adding strength to areas of the body that are susceptible to injury. Exercises that strengthen knees, shoulders, and elbows can also strengthen your game and keep you away from the emergency room. Weight training can also help to build strong wrists, which are necessary for completing a fast- paced rally of net shots. Although athletes in some sports need large bulky muscles in order to compete, this is not the case with badminton. A badminton player uses long, lean muscles that supply power and stamina, muscles that don't get in the way during a frenzied rally. Instead of short bursts of exercise with heavy barbells that build thick, bulky muscles, more repetitions with lighter weights are recommended.

Photo by Jeff Klemzak
Energetic badminton on a Sunday afternoon

Swimming as an exercise is not only fun but it also builds muscle and stamina. Long, steady laps using an overhand crawl stroke will build a strong endurance level. This can be followed for example, by shorter bursts of activity using a butterfly or breast stroke that will build shoulder, leg, and chest muscles. If you were to examine the physiques of Olympic swimmers, you would find them to be lean, strong, and supple. This is the same type of athletic build that one finds among competitive badminton players. Swimming enhances their health as well as their game.

Badminton is a sport that requires quick reflexes and solid hand-to-eye coordination. One way to improve such coordination is by juggling. That's right, juggling. It takes concentration, skill, and well-developed hand-to-eye coordination for two hands to keep three balls in motion. Some years ago, the popular screen actor, W.C. Fields, who once had been a vaudeville juggler, often amazed crowds with his skill at table tennis and his ability to read the label of a 78 rpm record while in motion on the turntable. He was able to accomplish these feats because of the unusually keen hand-to-eye coordination he had developed by practicing his juggling routines.

Nutrition

A good athlete not only trains and plays hard to get in shape for competition, but seeks good health through sensible eating. Even in the 1990s, not all Americans have discovered the benefits of a low fat/high fiber diet combined with aerobic exercise. The National Center for Health Statistics reports that one in three Americans is obese, with obesity defined as twenty percent or more above one's ideal weight. For example, a person whose normal weight is 150 pounds would be considered obese at 180 pounds.

The connection between nutrition and good health has been known to humans since ancient times. Professionals in the health field tell us that proper nutrition combined with exercise keeps our bodies in balance and our stamina level high. But what exactly is proper nutrition?

The most important nutrient is water. Remember that exercise dulls the thirst mechanism, especially in cooler weather. While you are exercising, thirst comes late, often after the body's fluid stores have been depleted. Therefore, it is important to constantly replenish the exercising body with liquid. You will feel better, especially during the exercise itself, if your fluid needs are met. The best fluid is plain, cool water—and is far better than soft drinks. Because it carries no refined sugar to slow the process, water quickly enters the muscle tissue quickly from the digestive tract to cool the body.

In addition, an energetic badminton player needs a diet rich in nutrients, rather than one designed only to satisfy cravings. A person playing competitive sports needs high-carbohydrate foods, such as fresh fruits, vegetables, and grains. The diet should be low in fat (well under twenty-five percent of the total calories) and provide an adequate supply of protein (ten to fifteen percent).

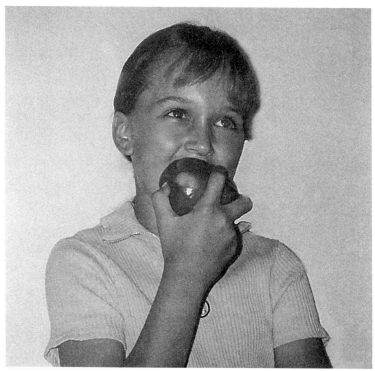

A crisp apple is a healthy snack

Protein is found in meat (not necessarily red meat), dairy products—such as cheese—and in certain food combinations such as rice and beans. A balanced diet also helps to keep one's weight within normal limits. Such a diet will reduce the risk of diabetes and heart disease, while supplying needed fiber and nutrients.

Most medical and nutritional experts agree that high cholesterol foods are based on animal products such as eggs, cheese, meats, milk, etc. The animal fat in these foods is very difficult for most people's bodies to process. In fact, fat is the single most difficult substance for the human body to digest. The cholesterol from animal products, when introduced to the body in large enough quantities, can adhere to the interior walls of the arteries. If the clogged arteries are those of the heart or brain, heart attacks and strokes can result. The popular belief that ardent, aerobic exercise neutralizes cholesterol in the bloodstream is a misconception. While it is true that exercise can effectively lower one's cholesterol rate, an overload of animal fat through the diet generally spells trouble for the circulatory system.

There will be times when an active athlete will need to adjust the high-fiber, high-carbohydrate, low-fat diet. Occasionally, during intensive training or play, the energy output can be so great that it exceeds the ability of the body to gain the calories it needs from food. In this case, sugar and fat can be added in the form of something relatively light, such as candy or a granola bar. Another occasion for diet adjustment is the pre-game meal. Foods rich in carbohydrates, such as pasta and fruit juices, are far better before a game than bulky, high-fiber foods. These exceptions are for athletes in training for serious competition rather than for those simply striving for fitness.

People in training for fitness or competition are better off avoiding "fast food" and any foods that are high in refined sugar and fat. Foods fried in fat such as potato chips, french fries, and dough-nuts are not part of a well-balanced diet. This advice is relevant for everyone, not just those in training. Often, young people acquiesce to peer pressure or cultural influences that advocate nutritiously poor foods. It is best to rely on education and good judgment when it comes to the important matters of diet, especially if you are participating in a competitive training program.

Tobacco and Alcohol

Tobacco use robs all body tissues of oxygen and nutrients and introduces damaging toxins into the body's systems. The use of cigarettes and other tobacco products virtually negates the beneficial effects of a healthful diet and exercise program. The ill effects of tobacco use are well known. Tobacco has been linked to cancer, emphysema, high blood pressure, heart disease, and many other maladies.

Alcoholic beverages, including beer, cause dehydration and introduce empty calories into the body. Alcohol contains seven calories per gram, almost as much as fat, but they are calories that fool the body into a feeling of satisfaction. In reality the calories obtained from beer and wine coolers are without value. Also, alcohol abuse puts unnecessary pressure on the body's filtration system, particularly the kidneys and liver. A competitive badminton player requires a well-cared-for, well-nourished body that has not been sabotaged by alcohol and tobacco.

Photo by Thumbs/Up

Competitive badminton requires optimum fitness

Physical fitness and skill at badminton—or any other sport—require hard work and dedication. It takes many hours on the practice court to develop into a ranked badminton player and many more to stay at that level. Even if your goal is just to play badminton for the sheer enjoyment of the game, exercise and proper nutrition are essential to get the most out of it, as well as to put you on the path to better fitness and good health.

☄ 6

SAFETY ON THE BADMINTON COURT

Although the badminton racquet and shuttlecock are fairly lightweight items, badminton players, because of the speed and intensity of the game, suffer their fair share of sports injuries. Constant shoulder and elbow motion, coupled with short bursts of running with sudden starts and stops, can overburden the body's joints and send a badminton player to the sidelines. When an injury occurs, it is always best to consult your doctor before embarking on any exercise regimen designed to overcome the sports injury.

Tennis Elbow

A common badminton injury is inflammation of the elbow, often referred to in the sports world as "tennis elbow." This is a nagging sort of injury that is aggravated by frequently using rotary motions of the forearm while holding something in the hand. Golfers and athletes who compete in racquet sports often complain of tennis elbow. The outside area of the elbow swells and aches, especially when it is put to use, making competition extremely difficult.

The suggested treatment for this condition is to rest the afflicted area, temporarily giving up badminton until the swelling and pain have subsided. It is also important to ice the elbow three times a day for thirty to sixty minutes during the early painful stage; then for fifteen minutes after activity has been resumed. Stretching exercises and physical therapy also are suggested as relief for the inflammation of tennis elbow. In more serious cases of tennis elbow, when simple painkillers are not sufficient, a doctor may administer a cortisone shot to the troubled area. This relieves the pain and can make physical therapy more effective. After a cortisone shot, however, an athlete should not play for at least two weeks.

As the pain of tennis elbow eventually lessens and the resumption of active play is considered, there are a few things that you can do to ease your way back into the sport. Always warm up carefully before you play. Put all of your major joints through a complete range of motion several times. Slowly go through all of the motions you use in your game. You might try to move your hand forward on the grip, giving the racquet a lighter feel to it. Also, try to avoid the shots for a while that tend to aggravate the condition. Reduce wrist motion as much as possible. You may need to take some lessons to learn to alter your strokes. A Velcro-secured forearm wrap can be worn just below the elbow to keep the vibration down and to ease the ache as you are playing. Finally, don't rush back into things. Start by playing a short amount of time as you regain your game, working up from a few rallies to a complete game.

Weak muscles are a major contributor to tennis elbow. Specific exercises can be beneficial to muscles that are associated with the inflamed tendons. These exercises may be done after the initial painful period has passed, or you may do them as preventive maintenance, strengthening the muscles before they become injured.

Elbow Stretch

Hold your racquet arm at shoulder level straight out from your body. Clench your fist, then flex your wrist downward as far as possible. Return the wrist to a neutral position, then alternately rotate the arm inward with a flexed wrist, then rotate the arm outward with an extended wrist (so that you can see the back of your hand). Ten repetitions twice a day are recommended for each exercise.

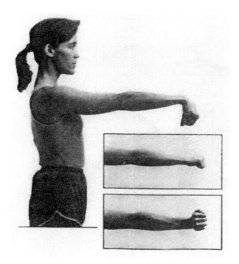

Elbow Stretch

Wrist Curls

While seated, rest your forearm on a tabletop with the elbow down. Place a rolled-up towel under your arm near the wrist to act as a fulcrum. Hold a one pound weight (or an unopened can of soup) in

Wrist Curls

your hand and slowly raise your wrist as high as you can. Do this exercise first with the palm up, then with the palm down. As your strength increases, gradually increase the weight of the object.

Squeezing

Squeeze a rubber ball to strengthen the inflamed area. Use a ball that is approximately the size of a racquet ball (note that rubber balls are available in various densities). Use one that is easy to squeeze so that the benefit of this exercise is not lost.

Squeezing

Twisting

With your arms outstretched, try wringing out a heavy towel with both of your hands. This twisting exercise will both strengthen the muscles of the forearm, and ultimately reduce the stress on your elbows.

Twisting

Shoulder Problems

Shoulder pain is a very common ailment among badminton players. On the court, a fall is the most likely way of receiving a shoulder injury, although shoulder problems can develop gradually from years of overhead shots. If a fall causes a dislocation of the shoulder joint, you may have earned a ticket to the emergency room. Shoulder pain that develops into instability of the joint can be treated by an orthopedic specialist. Usually, the treatment includes avoidance of the overhead shots that aggravate the problem, treating any associated bursitis, and strengthening the rotator cuff with a series of shoulder exercises.

Other Injuries

Achilles tendon problems, as well as knee and ankle injuries, frequently occur among badminton players. Proper foot and ankle mechanics, demonstrated by an experienced badminton coach, can keep the wrong thing from happening on the badminton court. A good training schedule combined with strength exercises can also minimize the frequency of debilitating injuries.

Strength Training

A balanced training program includes running for aerobic fitness, weight training for strength, and skill acquisition for dexterity in badminton. A combination of all three training regimes produces a fit athlete who is skilled at the sport he or she has chosen. Not only should the training program be balanced, but there should be balance within the weight training or strength program as well. The human muscular system is arranged in pairs so that as one muscle performs a particular action, another muscle or muscle group does the opposite. For example, as you hold your arm out from your body with a racquet in your hand you can feel the extensor muscles in the forearm tighten as the triceps, between the elbow and the shoulder, grow slack. All of the muscles in the arm need to be trained to complete the necessary badminton shots, not just half of them.

First Aid

As you are preparing for a badminton match, try to remember to keep a well-supplied first aid kit close by. Accidents can happen on the badminton court and it is best to be prepared when they do. Cuts and bruises can occur from falls. Players are sometimes struck by mishandled racquets. Ankles, wrists, and knees are sprained occasion-ally during the frenzied play that can occur on the court. A first aid kit should contain gauze and strip bandages, aspirin, scissors, tweezers, adhesive tape, ace bandages, and a cold pack.

An ice bucket should be kept adjacent to the badminton court, but not just to store juices and soft drinks. If a sprained ankle is quickly immersed in ice water, swelling can be kept to a minimum and the damaged joint will respond to treatment more rapidly than if nothing had been done.

Some years ago, a small group of friends began to play a game of doubles in a park in Northern California. Through the tree-lined park flowed a stream that carried the runoff from the snow-packed mountains nearby. During some vigorous net play, one of the men in the group sprained his ankle. His friends helped him remove his shoe, then carried him the short distance to the icy stream where he immersed his foot. Later, at the emergency room, the group was congratulated by the attending doctor for their quick thinking and for saving their friend from unnecessary complications. Not every badminton court has a cold stream nearby, so keep that ice bucket handy.

7

YOUTH & AMATEUR BADMINTON

High School Badminton

Young people who are interested in badminton will find many opportunities to advance to a structured, competitive level. High school campuses across the United States offer badminton as part of the physical education program. In fact, many Americans who play badminton on a regular basis were introduced to the sport by their high school physical education coach.

Athletic programs in the secondary schools are directed by state agencies or federations. Regulations that govern them vary from state to state. In California, the California Interscholastic Federation (C.I.F.) sets the rules for high school athletics.

The C.I.F. also has designated geographic divisions within states and it divides the schools, for purposes of athletic competition, by enroll-

ment size and other factors. Generally, badminton is treated as a Spring sport, played from
February to June and, in California, the teams are
formed on a coed basis. In many other areas of
the country, oddly enough, badminton teams are
restricted to females only.

Photo by Jeff Klemzak
A mixed doubles match in a high school gymnasium

A typical high school badminton program begins
with two weeks devoted to running and learning
the basic strokes. After the new team members
are familiar with the mechanics of the drop, the
smash, the backcourt clear, and the strategies
employed, a few cuts are made to pare the team
down to size. In two more weeks, after the team
has drilled in the basics and become better
conditioned through exercise and intra-squad

games, the team is ready for interscholastic matches.

A high school with an enrollment of 2,000 students can usually field a varsity team of twenty-four athletes—twelve girls and twelve boys. Depending upon the location and size of nearby schools, matches are generally held twice a week. High school programs use the format that has become familiar in established tournament play; i.e., the complement of singles and doubles matches for males and females and, of course, the popular mixed doubles matches that are unique to badminton.

Unfortunately, at this time only seven states offer high school badminton programs. They are California, Arizona, Florida, Illinois, Maryland, Minnesota, and New York. Badminton clubs, however, are springing up all over the country as badminton grows ever more popular. In a few years, high school athletic associations will begin to include programs for badminton in order to train the youthful athletes who demand them.

Badminton Clubs

Aspiring and established badminton players in various urban areas throughout the country are fortunate if they live near private badminton clubs. Private clubs offer coaching and skills clinics, and often provide the arena for tournament play. Some clubs feature drop-in programs, loosely structured events that encourage members from one club to drop in on the members of another for a day or an evening of badminton matches. Events such as these are usually conducted without the benefit of umpires, and players perform on the honor system, calling their own lines and faults.

Youth Programs

With the help of various badminton equipment manufacturers, badminton coaches have instituted youth programs in Southern California to broaden the opportunities of players and coaches alike—and to develop their skills within the sport of badminton.

Based on the efforts of local badminton coaches within the ranks of the Southern California Badminton Association (SCBA), area high schools have opened their gymnasiums one night a week to willing athletes.

School boards had been reluctant to offer evening programs in the past because of problems in obtaining affordable accident insurance. USA Badminton, however, has forged ahead to locate insurance coverage for these evening athletic programs, which now have become a reality. USA Badminton, in order to provide the insurance coverage, requires players to form a local badminton club and become members of USA Badminton.

The HL Corporation, a California racquet manufacturer, is sponsoring a series of high school exhibitions that are designed to encourage interest in badminton. This program sends alumni to their former high schools to engage in badminton matches that demonstrate the finer points of the game. The demonstrations are designed to recruit athletes to the sport of badminton and to motivate the schools to include badminton in their athletic programs.

Photo by Jeff Klemzak
Court action at a badminton club

Four tournaments, held from October through January since 1995, before the start of the high school badminton season, are played by high school-age badminton players. These annual tournaments follow a regular circuit in Southern California, visiting different cities, showcasing fine young badminton talent along the way. All of the equipment necessary for the matches and the awards is donated by Yonex. Programs such as the campus exhibitions and the Yonex Prep Badminton Tournament Circuit are one day expected—with perseverence and devotion to the sport—to put badminton on par with tennis and other extracurricular sports programs at the high school level.

The most far-reaching program initiated by SCBA volunteers to further the sport on the junior level includes clinics for players and coaches and one that eventually will find and develop some of the best badminton talent in the country.

Three summer day camps have been created for high school-age badminton players. Two of the camps are set up for players of intermediate skill and one camp is for advanced or elite players. The goal of the advanced day camp is to send as many skilled players as possible to the Olympic Training Center in Colorado Springs, Colorado. The SCBA volunteers created a roster of coaches in the Southern California area who provided a two-day coaching clinic in August 1997 to enhance the number of USA Badminton certificated coaches. To further upgrade the quality of American badminton coaching, the International Badminton Federation (IBF) underwrote the expense of bringing foreign coaches to the United States to assist at the coaching clinic.

An SCBA committee of five coaches has been formed to select a list of players deemed worthy by their mentors of eventually filling the rosters of elite junior badminton teams. The coaches reevaluate the list on the basis of tournament results and other factors three times per season. After the California Interscholastic Federation (CIF) finals each May, the panel of coaches selects four teams of fourteen boys and girls, to create a group of all-stars from four areas around the state. This group participates in the Southern California Prep All-Star Badminton Team Championships over a two-day period. These athletes are high school seniors who participate in singles, doubles, and mixed doubles play.

Photo by Jeff Klemzak

A prep star waits for the serve

The athletes attend an awards banquet after the tournament to receive medals they have earned. From this group, two winners of the Most Valuable Player Award are chosen, one male and one female, to receive advanced training anywhere they choose in the United States. Included in the award are housing expenses and a per diem to accommodate the expenses of their advanced training.

Photo by Jeff Klemzak

A badminton club manager provides equipment, a place to play, and plenty of friendly advice

The junior badminton program in Miller Place, New York has been producing star athletes for several years. The Miller Place Badminton Club provides training for beginner and intermediate players while the more advanced students compete on the high school varsity team.

In addition to the California youth programs, the summer camp program sponsored by the Miller Place Badminton Club prepares young athletes for competition at the Junior National Badminton Championships. The program in New York is so strong that in recent years one-third of all the participants at the Junior Nationals have come from Miller Place. Since the badminton program began there in the mid-1970s, Miller Place athletes participating in the Junior Nationals have been awarded 118 gold medals.

The record of high school varsity badminton teams is even more impressive. Since the first badminton varsity squad was formed at Miller Place High School in 1973, the team has won 372 consecutive matches—representing no defeats in twenty-four consecutive seasons. *It is the longest winning streak for any team participating in any sport, amateur or professional, in the United States.*

In 1997, Miller Place sent three of their young athletes to the Olympic Training Center in Colorado Springs, Colorado.

The goal of all of these programs is to continually upgrade the quality of badminton play in the United States and to field a world-class team for the Summer Olympic Games. The sincerity of the coaches and players and the hard work of administrators within the USAB, the IBF, and other organizations is apparent as badminton gains popularity on a worldwide basis and moves into the 21st century as a major sport.

Howard Bach

Starting out as a 6-year-old swatting the shuttle back and forth over the net with his father, Howard was one of many pint-sized athletes in those days at the San Francisco YMCA. Now, with ten Junior National Championships under his belt, Howard Bach has his sights set on a gold medal at the Summer Olympic Games in Sidney in 2000.

Howard came into his own as a singles player in 1996 with victories in the Manhattan Beach Junior Open in California and at the Pan American Junior Championships held in San Juan, Puerto Rico. At Manhattan Beach, Howard defeated Taipei's Fang-Chi Wu in a stirring battle that thrilled the crowd with its intensity.

Howard is currently a resident athlete at the U.S. Olympic Training Center at Colorado Springs, Colorado.

"My dad always wanted me to go to the Olympics," Howard says, "and hopefully I can make his dream a reality."

Photo by Jim Stabler
Howard Bach—An intense young athlete in tournament play

8

PLAYING BADMINTON AT HOME

If you are interested in learning to play badminton, but don't yet feel committed enough to go out for the high school team or to join a private club, you may try to get set up either in your yard at home or at a nearby park. A well-stocked sporting goods store can supply you with racquets, nets, shuttles, and a rule book to help you get started.

If you are planning to play on a grassy surface, you can lay out the court with some cord or heavy twine. Duct tape works rather well if you set up on a paved surface. The court should be approximately twenty feet wide and forty-four feet long with defined short- and long-service lines. (See the court diagram in Chapter 3.) The net will divide the court in half and a center line should be added from the short service line to the rear boundary.

Look for a place that is free from low overhead power lines (you may need to trim a tree limb or two). Remember that windy days can play havoc with the temperamental nature of the shuttle. The best back yards for badminton are those that are lined with trees, which provide shade and act as buffers against the wind. A surface of short, durable grass in solid, pothole-free, flat soil is also desirable. Some dogs love to chase an errant shuttle, so keep Fido tied up while you are playing.

Photo by Jeff Klemzak
A front-yard match in the shade

Setting up a badminton court near an active bee-hive also is not a very good idea. One badminton enthusiast tells a story of a group of friends who put up a net and staked out boundary lines in a shaded park in a large western city. The game progressed and as play became increasingly intense, a clear shot to the back boundary of the opponents' court was struck a trifle too hard, causing the shuttle to sail into a tree and strike a wasps' nest. The insects, enraged at having their home violated, dive-bombed the badminton party and sent the players running for cover.

Photo by Jeff Klemzak
Badminton is a sport for people of all ages

Badminton can provide a lifetime of enjoyment. It is common to see people of all ages competing on the badminton court, including those who are well into their seventies. As a spectator sport, badminton offers plenty of fast-paced action, combined with deft athletic maneuvering that enthralls an audience. Badminton is available to

practically anyone who wishes to pursue it and is
health-promoting to those who play it. But above
all, badminton is fun.

Photo by Jeff Klemzak

Badminton is great family fun

9

BADMINTON ETIQUETTE

1. Loud, abusive, or profane language, racquet throwing or hitting the shuttle indiscriminately are prohibited.

2. Be courteous to other players at all times.

3. Retrieve the shuttle at the end of a rally when it has fallen on your side of the net and promptly return it to your opponent.

4. When there is no umpire, call out the score before each service.

5. When there are no line judges, always make fair, quick and accurate line calls. If in doubt, give your opponent the benefit.

6. After losing, acknowledge your opponent's strength.

7. Do not walk behind or beside a court while the shuttle is in play.

In Tournament

1. Send all entries in well before the deadline.

2. Do not withdraw from a tournament after the draw has been made or default in a tournament except for illness, injury, or personal emergency.

3. Be on court promptly when matches are called.

4. Restrict on-court warmups to the permitted time.

5. Accept the decisions of opponents and officials.

6. Thank the umpire and service judge after all matches and thank the organizers before leaving the tournament.

10

WHERE TO PLAY

Region 1—Northeast

Connecticut

Bloomfield
  Greater Hartford Badminton Club
Danbury
  Greater Danbury Badminton
Farmington
  Farmington Badminton Club
Farmington
  Return of Serve Badminton Club
Granby
  Granby Recreation
Greenwich
  Greenwich Badminton Club
Greenwich
  Greenwich Boys and Girls Club
Madison
  Madison Badminton Club
New Haven
  Yale Badminton Club

Newington
    Newington Badminton Club
Old Lyme
    Lyme-Old Lyme Middle School Club
Orange
    Orange Badminton Club
Orange
    The Badminton Club of New Haven
Ridgefield
    Ridgefield Badminton Club
Simsbury
    Simsbury Badminton Club
Trumbull
    Trumbull Recreation Department
    (limited to Trumbull residents only)
Westport
    Westport/Weston YMCA

Delaware

Newcastle
    Newcastle Badminton Club

District of Columbia

Washington
    Badminton Club of D.C.
    Geo. Washington University Badminton Club
    Pentagon Athletic Club (POAC) (restricted to
    members and guests)

Maine

Falmouth
  Portland Athletic Club

Maryland

Baltimore
  Loch Raven Badminton Club
College Park
  Badminton Club at the University of Maryland
  (open to university students, employees, and
  alumni only)
Owings Mills
  Garrison Forest High School Badminton Club
Potomac
  Badminton Club of D.C.
  Bauer Drive Recreation Center
  Montgomery County Badminton Club

Massachusetts

Boston
  The University Club of Boston
Cambridge
  Harvard Badminton Club
  MIT Badminton Club
Dorchester
  Irish Club
Duxbury
  Duxbury Bay Badminton Club
Hamilton
  Hamilton/Wenham Badminton Club

Marblehead
    Gut 'n' Feathers Club
Needham
    Park and Recreation Badminton Club
North Dartmouth
    The Bird and Bottle Club
Northhampton
    Smith College
Salem
    Salem State College
Wellesley
    Maugus Club (private club)
Westfield
    Westfield Badminton Club
Winchester
    Winchester Badminton Club

New Hampshire

Concord
    Racquet Club of Concord

New Jersey

Bloomingdale
    Bloomingdale Badminton Club
Livingston
    Livingston Badminton Club
Long Valley
    Washington Township Badminton Club
Mountain Lakes
    Mountain Lakes Badminton Club

New Brunswick
    Rutgers University Badminton Club

New York

Amherst
    UB Badminton Club
Bayside
    Queensborough Community College
    Badminton Club
Brooklyn
    Brooklyn Badminton Club
Buffalo
    Badminton Club of Greater Buffalo
Garden City
    Garden City Badminton Club
Huntington Station
    Walt Whitman Badminton Club
Miller Place
    Miller Place Badminton Club
New York City
    Badminton Club of the City of New York
    Central Manhattan Badminton Club
    Columbia University (club open to university
    students, employees, and alumni only)
    New York Athletic Club/Badminton Club
    (restricted to members and guests)
    United Nations Badminton Club
Northport
    Northport Badminton Club
Rochester
    University of Rochester Badminton Club

Stony Brook
    Stony Brook Badminton Association
Williamsville
    Town of Amherst Recreation Department
    Badminton Club

Pennsylvania

Bryn Mawr
    Bryn Mawr College Badminton Club
    Harcum College
    Main Line Badminton Club
Carlisle
    Carlisle Badminton Club
Gettysburg
    Gettysburg College
Kimberton
    Kimberton Badminton Club
Mansfield
    Mansfield University Badminton Club
Narberth
    Haverford Club
Nottingham
    Pittwillow Badminton Club
Philadelphia
    Drexel Badminton Club
Philadelphia
    University of Pennsylvania Badminton Club
    (University affiliation only)
Pittsburgh
    Carnegie Mellon University

Reading
    Albright College Badminton Club
State College
    Penn State Badminton Club
Swathmore
    Swarthmore College Badminton Club
West Chester
    The Fitness Business

Rhode Island

Block Island
    Block Island Badminton Club

Vermont

Brattleboro
    Southern Vermont Badminton Club

Virginia

Arlington
    City of Arlington Recreation Department
Fairfax
    Virginia Badminton Club
Manasses
    Sports Network
Virginia Beach
    Virginia Beach Badminton League
Williamsburg
    College of William and Mary Badminton Club

Region 2—Midwest

Illinois

Arlington Heights
  Forest View Badminton Club

Carbondale
  Southern Illinois Badminton Club

Champaign
  Illini Badminton Intercollegiate Sport Club

Chicago
  McKinley Badminton Club

Chicago
  University of Chicago Badminton Club

Downers Grove
  Chi-Town Badminton Club

Evanston
  Evanston Badminton Club

Mt. Prospect
  Park Ridge Badminton Club

Villa Park
  Willowbrook Badminton Club

Indiana

Indianapolis
  Indianapolis Badminton Club

Martinsville
  Race Badminton Club

Iowa

Ames
   Iowa State University Badminton Club

Kentucky

Louisville
   Louisville Badminton Club
   University of Louisville Badminton Club

Michigan

Benton Harbor
   Lake Michigan College Badminton Club
Birmingham
   Birmingham Badminton Club
Dearborn
   Dearborn Westwood Badminton Club
East Lansing
   Michigan State University Badminton Club
Flint
   Flint Badminton Club
Grosse Pointe
   Grosse Pointe Badminton Association
Kalamazoo
   Kalamazoo Badminton Club

Minnesota

Minneapolis/St. Paul
   Minneapolis Athletic Club (private)
   Minnesota State Badminton Association
   Decathalon Club

Midway YMCA
Northwest Racquet, Swim & Health Club
Minnetonka Recreation
Woodbury Group

Missouri

St. Louis
Gateway Badminton Club
River City Badminton Club
St. Louis Badminton Club

Nebraska

Papillion
Top Flight Badminton Club

Ohio

Cincinnati
B&B Badminton Club
Dayton
Sinclair Badminton Club
Shaker Heights
Shaker Heights Badminton Club
Toledo
Toledo Badminton Club
University of Toledo Badminton Club
Wooster
The College of Wooster Badminton Club

Wisconsin

Madison
  Triple B Badminton Club
  University of Wisconsin Badminton Club
Milwaukee
  Greater Milwaukee Badminton Club
  Milwaukee Athletic Club

Region 3—Southeast

Florida

Bradenton
  Bradenton Strikers
  Brandon Badminton Club
Miami Lakes
  Miami Badminton Club
St. Petersburg
  St. Petersburg YMCA
Tampa
  Sun Coast Badminton Club

Georgia

Atlanta
  Atlanta Athletic Club
  Georgia State University Badminton Club
  Spelman Badminton Club
Oxford
  Oxford University Badminton Club
  (University affiliation only)

Louisiana

Baton Rouge
  Baton Rouge Badminton Club
New Orleans
  New Orleans Badminton Club
Shreveport
  Shreveport Badminton Club

North Carolina

Asheville
  Asheville Badminton Club
Charlotte
  Charlotte Badminton Club

Oklahoma

Norman
  University of Oklahoma Badminton Club
Ponca City
  Conco Badminton Club

South Carolina

Columbia
  Palmetto Badminton Club

Tennessee

Bristol
  King College
Memphis
  Memphis Badminton Club

Nashville
  Nashville Badminton Club

Texas

Abilene
  Abilene Christian University
Austin
  University of Texas Badminton Club
Belton
  University of Mary Hardin Baylor Club
College Station
  Texas A&M Badminton Club
Dallas
  North Dallas Badminton Association
Denton
  University of North Texas Badminton Club
Houston
  Houston Badminton Association
Richardson
  Huffines Recreation Center
San Antonio
  San Antonio Badminton Club
Waco
  Baylor University Badminton Club (University
  affiliation only; guests permitted)

Region 4—Northwest

Alaska

Anchorage
  Anchorage Badminton Club

Fairbanks
Fairbanks Badminton Club

Colorado

Colorado Springs
Pikes Peak Badminton Club
Denver
Denver Athletic Club (private club)

Oregon

Eugene
University of Oregon Club Sports
Portland
Multnomah Athletic Club (private club)
Salem
YMCA of Salem

Washington

Bellevue
Bellevue Boys Club
Bellingham
Western Washington University
Mercer Island
Mercer Island Parks and Recreation
SeaTac
North SeaTac Park Community Group
Seattle
Highline Badminton Club
Meadowbrook Community Center
Northwest Badminton Club

Spokane
Spokane Badminton and Pickleball Club
Tacoma
Tacoma Badminton Club

Region 5—Southwest

Arizona

Prescott
Prescott High School Badminton Club
Phoenix
Phoenix YMCA

California
Northern California Badminton Association

Berkeley
UC Berkeley Badminton Club
Davis
University of California at Davis Badminton
Club
Hayward
California State University Club
Los Gatos
Los Gatos Recreation Badminton Club
Mendocino
Mendocino Badminton Club
Menlo Park
Menlo Park Recreation Department
Palo Alto
Penninsula Badminton Club

Pleasant Hill
    Pleasant Hill Adult Center Group
Oakland
    Bret Harte Junior High Group
Sacramento
    Sacramento State University Group
San Francisco
    Birds of a Feather Club
San Francisco
    South San Francisco High School Group
San Jose
    Camden Badminton Club
Stanford
    Stanford Badminton Club (University
    affiliation only)
Stockton
    Franklin High Badminton Club
Stockton
    St. Mary's High School
Suisan
    Solono Community College Badminton Club
Sunnyvale
        Sunnyvale Badminton Club

Southern California Badminton Association

Arcadia
    Arcadia Badminton Club
Baldwin Park
    Baldwin Park High School Group
Burbank
    Burbank Badminton Club

Colton
  Manhattan Beach Club
El Monte
  San Gabriel Valley Badminton Club
Garden Grove
  Garden Grove Badminton Club
Glendale
  Glendale Badminton Club
Hollywood
  Hollywood YMCA Group
Huntington Beach
  Seahawk Badminton Club
Irvine
  University of California at Irvine Badminton
  Club
Laguna Hills
  Badminton Club of Leisure World (private)
Long Beach
  Long Beach Badminton Club
Los Angeles
  Mar Vista Park Group
  Thai Badminton Club
  UCLA Badminton Club
Manhattan Beach
  Manhattan Beach Badminton Club (private)
Orange
  Orange County Badminton Club
San Diego
  San Diego Badminton Club
Santa Ana
  Santa Ana High School Badminton Club

Santa Monica
    Santa Monica College Badminton
Ventura County
    Ventura County Group
Westchester
    Westchester Badminton Club

Hawaii

Hilo
    Hilo Badminton Club
Honolulu
    Hawaii Badminton Club

Nevada

Las Vegas
    Thee Badminton Club

New Mexico

Las Cruces
    Mesilla Valley Badminton Club
Socorro
    New Mexico Tech Badminton Club

Utah

Salt Lake City
    University of Utah Badminton Club

GLOSSARY

Alley—Extension of the court by 1-1/2 feet on both sides for doubles play.

Backcourt—Back third of the court near the rear boundary line.

Backhand—A stroke hit on the left side of the body by a right-handed player and vice versa.

Balk—Any deceptive movement that is disruptive to an opponent, either before or during a serve, also called a feint.

Baseline—The back boundary line at each end of the court.

Bird—Also known as the shuttlecock or shuttle.

Carry—An illegal tactic, also called a sling or a throw, where the shuttle is caught and held on the racquet, then slung during the execution of the stroke.

Center Line—A line perpendicular to the net that separates the left and right service courts.

Clear—A stroke that lofts the shuttle to the back of the opponent's court. A high clear is a defensive shot while the flatter, attacking clear is a offensive maneuver.

Drive—A stroke that clears the net in a low trajectory at a high rate of speed.

Drop—A shot hit softly so as to barely clear the net and drop sharply on the opponent's side.

False starts—An illegal, deceptive move on the part of the server. Service must be straightforward. Once the motion to serve has begun it must follow through.

Fault—A violation of the playing rules that results in a point or forfeiture of the serve.

Feints—Legal trickery. For example, fast-charging the shuttle, then striking it softly to confuse one's opponent. This change of motion is prohibited, however, while serving.

Finesse Players—Players who rely on lobs, feints, foot-speed and court position in their offensive game, as opposed to those who strike the shuttle with power.

Flick—A quick movement of the wrist that sends the shuttle to the rear of the opponent's court. A surprise move to an opponent who is expecting a softer shot.

Forecourt—The front portion of the court, between the net and the short service line.

Forehand—A stroke hit on the right side by a right-handed player.

Game—Fifteen points for men and 11 points for women in singles play, 15 points for doubles matches.

Hairpin Net Shot—This is a shot made from near and below the net. The shuttle rises, just clears the net then drops suddenly on the other side. The flight of the shuttle resembles the shape of a hairpin.

Halfcourt Shot—A shot hit low, as a line drive in baseball, that lands in midcourt between the opposing players in a doubles match.

Handicap Competition—This is the top level of badminton play. Players in this division participate in tournaments; i.e., the U.S. Open, etc.

In—When the shuttle stays in bounds and remains in play.

In Play—The shuttle is in play when it has been properly served and remains in bounds.

Kill—A fast, downward shot that cannot be returned; a put-away.

Let—The official stops play in order to replay the rally.

Long Service Line—The back boundary line in singles. In doubles, a line 2-1/2 feet inside the back boundary line. The serve must not cross this line.

Love—In scoring, nothing or zero.

Match—Best two out of three games to determine the winner.

Mixed Doubles—A male and female play as partners in a four-handed game.

Net Players—In doubles or mixed doubles play, the position of the net player is in the forecourt.

Net Shot—A shot struck near the net that drops sharply, clearing the net.

Power Players—Players who rely on driving the shuttle over the net with as much force as they can muster. Remember, the shuttle can reach speeds of up to 200 miles per hour.

Put-Away—Same as a kill.

Racquet—Used by the player to strike the shuttle. Weighs three ounces and is twenty-seven inches long. Made of ceramic or graphite, strung with gut or synthetic fibers.

Rally—An exchange of shots between opponents.

Referee—The senior official at a badminton tournament.

Round-the-Head—An overhand smash shot, using a forehand grip from the vicinity of the left shoulder by a right-handed player.

Serve—The stroke used to put the shuttle in play.

Service Court—The area where the serve must be made.

Setting—When the score is tied at 13, for example, the player who first reached the score of 13 has the option of extending the game beyond the limit of 15 points to 18. This is done to stall an opponent who has mounted a rally.

Short-Service Line—A line 6-1/2 feet from the net that the serve must reach.

Shuttlecock—The object struck by the racquet. Made from goose feathers and cork or from nylon.

Smash—An overhand power shot that forces the shuttle downward over the net. The primary attack stroke in badminton.

Umpire—The umpire enforces the rules of play in a badminton match. If a referee is also present at the match, the umpire reports to the referee.

Unsighted—When an umpire's view of a play in question is blocked, the umpire is termed "unsighted."

Wood Shot—Striking the cork base of the shuttle with the racquet frame. A legal shot since 1963.

USA Badminton (USAB) is the national governing body for badminton as recognized by the United States Olympic Committee (USOC) and the International Badminton Federation (IBF).

Each year USAB sanctions hundreds of local, regional, and national tournaments, as well as the U.S. Open International event, for players of all ages and skill levels.

As a member of USA Badminton, you receive:

- A USAB membership card—your passport to play in sanctioned events, including top-level national competitions.
- The latest information through USAB publications.
- A USBA decal to proudly display your affiliation.
- Event notices.
- Special deals on exclusive apparel, merchandise, and videos.

- New skills through training and certification programs for coaches and umpires.
- Opportunities to improve your play and to gain instruction through regional and national training camps.
- Discounts on rental cars and airline tickets.
- A chance to become a member of an Olympic, Pan American, World, or U.S. Olympic Festival team through the trials selection process.
- Liability insurance during competitions.
- A voice in USBA leadership through your vote (for members 18 and older).

To join, call the USBA at
(719) 578-4808
or write to:

United States Badminton Association
One Olympic Plaza
Colorado Springs, CO 80909

United States Olympic Committee
Sports Series Order Form
(Please print):

Date:_____

Name: _____

Address: _____

City:_____State:____Zip: ____

Phone:(___) _____

Title	*Price*	*Qty / Amount*
A Basic Guide to Archery	$7.95	___/_____
A Basic Guide to Badminton	*$7.95*	___/_____
A Basic Guide to Cycling	$7.95	___/_____
A Basic Guide to Decathlon	$8.95	___/_____
A Basic Guide to Equestrian	$7.95	___/_____
A Basic Guide to Soccer	$7.95	___/_____
A Basic Guide to Wrestling	$7.95	___/_____
Olympism	$8.95	___/_____

Subtotal: _____

8.25% tax (CA only): _____

S/H: _____

Total: _____

S/H charges:
1 title $2.50
each additional title $1.00

Send this order form with payment (check, money order or credit card info), to the address at the right.

Griffin Publishing
544 W. Colorado Street
Glendale, CA 91204

Credit cards: VISA or MasterCard only.
(circle one) **VISA   MC**

Account number _____

Expiration date ___/___

Signature _____

For faster service on credit card orders call 1-818-244-1470
or Fax 1-818-244-7408.